Well-being in the Workplace

A guide to resilience for individuals and teams

Well-being in the Workplace

A guide to resilience for individuals and teams

SARAH COOK

IT Governance Publishing

Every possible effort has been made to ensure that the information contained in this book is accurate at the time of going to press, and the publisher and the author cannot accept responsibility for any errors or omissions, however caused. Any opinions expressed in this book are those of the author, not the publisher. Websites identified are for reference only, not endorsement, and any website visits are at the reader's own risk. No responsibility for loss or damage occasioned to any person acting, or refraining from action, as a result of the material in this publication can be accepted by the publisher or the author.

Apart from any fair dealing for the purposes of research or private study, or criticism or review, as permitted under the Copyright, Designs and Patents Act 1988, this publication may only be reproduced, stored or transmitted, in any form, or by any means, with the prior permission in writing of the publisher or, in the case of reprographic reproduction, in accordance with the terms of licences issued by the Copyright Licensing Agency. Enquiries concerning reproduction outside those terms should be sent to the publisher at the following address:

IT Governance Publishing Ltd
Unit 3, Clive Court
Bartholomew's Walk
Cambridgeshire Business Park
Ely, Cambridgeshire
CB7 4EA
United Kingdom
www.itgovernancepublishing.co.uk

The authors have asserted their rights of the author under the Copyright, Designs and Patents Act, 1988, to be identified as the authors of this work.

First edition published in the United Kingdom in 2021 by IT Governance Publishing

ISBN 978-1-78778-316-4

PREFACE

This book is aimed at managers who need to build resilience in both themselves and their team and improve their own and others' well-being. It will help you learn the best ways to develop your own resilience and that of others.

I have written this book at a time of a global pandemic and increasing uncertainty at work. As COVID-19 continues to affect people's health and well-being, managers need not only to build the resilience of their team, but also to remain strong and bounce back when adversity impacts them.

Many people today struggle with job and/or financial insecurity. Change and uncertainty are now the norm. With more people encouraged to work from home, there is increased risk of isolation and it can be hard for managers to manage their own emotions as well as those of their team.

This book provides practical tips and advice. It will help you recognise the impact ambiguity can have on well-being and identify the signs of declining mental, physical, emotional and social well-being. It is also a useful guide to equip managers with the skills and confidence to effectively build their own and others' resilience and support their team's well-being.

The good news is that in reading this book, you have taken a positive step towards building your own and your team's resilience. I hope the book enables you to identify concrete actions you can take to build well-being. The challenge is to turn these actions into resolutions that stick. When you embed your intended actions in repeatable behaviours that become habits, you'll increase your own and your team's ability to bounce back.

Sarah Cook

Managing Director, The Stairway Consultancy Ltd

www.thestairway.co.uk

ABOUT THE AUTHOR

Sarah Cook is the Managing Director of The Stairway Consultancy Ltd. She has more than 20 years' consulting experience, specialising in leadership and management development. Before this, Sarah worked for Unilever and as head of customer care for a retail marketing consultancy.

Sarah has practical experience helping managers build their own and team members' resilience and create high-performing teams. She has also worked extensively with team members to help them effectively increase their personal well-being.

Sarah is a business author and has written widely on leadership, management development, team building and coaching. She also speaks regularly at conferences and seminars on these topics.

Sarah is a Chartered Fellow of the Chartered Institute of Personnel Development and a Chartered Marketer. She has an MA from the University of Cambridge and an MBA from The Open University. Sarah is an accredited user of a wide range of psychometric and team diagnostic tools.

For more information about The Stairway Consultancy, please see _www.thestairway.co.uk_ or contact _sarah@thestairway.co.uk_.

Learn more about Sarah's other publications by visiting: _www.itgovernancepublishing.co.uk/author/sarah-cook_.

ACKNOWLEDGEMENTS

This book is based on best-practice guidelines for developing resilience and enhancing well-being. The following organisations were valuable sources of reference:

Chartered Institute of Personnel Development:
www.cipd.co.uk

Heads Together: *www.headstogether.org.uk*

Mind UK: *www.mind.org.uk*

NHS: *www.nhs.uk/conditions/stress-anxiety-depression*

BBC News Headroom:
www.bbc.co.uk/programmes/articles/YfRzhXDKSZQxFVn 30TlXBj/your-mental-health-toolkit

Mayo Clinic: *www.mayoclinic.org*

I would also like to thank the following reviewers for their helpful feedback during the production of this book:

- Rebecca Fisher: Volunteering Co-ordinator/Conservation Assistant;
- Rob Ford: Senior ITSM Consultant;
- Debbie Larson: MSc Occupational Therapist, Mindfulness Based Cognitive Therapy Teacher;
- Sophie Sayer: Sales Director and Joint Managing Executive of IT Governance Publishing; and

Acknowledgements

- Vicki Utting: Managing Executive of IT Governance Publishing.

DISCLAIMER

All names quoted in this book are fictitious and have been presented for learning, understanding and explaining purposes only.

CONTENTS

Contents

Contents

CHAPTER 1: WHAT IS RESILIENCE?

Introduction

If you are reading this book, my assumption is that you want to increase your own resilience and potentially that of your team. In this chapter, I define resilience and discuss the need for resilience during and after the COVID-19 pandemic. I discuss the characteristics of resilient professionals and the link between resilience and well-being, focusing on physical, emotional, mental and social health.

What is resilience?

Resilience is the ability to cope with setbacks and find solutions to problems. It is the ability to bounce back from adversity and hardships, learn from the experience and move on. Being resilient means having the strength and conviction to confront life's challenges.

Resilient people experience suffering, stress and emotional upheaval, but they are able to work through it and adapt positively to difficult circumstances. Here are two examples:

The expeditioner Sir Ernest Shackleton aimed to be the first person to cross 1,500 miles of the Antarctic tundra. In 1914, Shackleton's ship was stuck in ice for nearly 11 months and eventually sank. The crew escaped in lifeboats and rowed for a week before reaching a deserted island. However, Shackleton realised he would need to return to their last port of call, a whaling station on an island 800 miles away, to get help. He and part of his crew rowed for 17 days to reach the island, only to realise that the whaling station was on the other side. They walked for 36 hours in deep snow to reach the station. They were able to rescue the rest of the crew, and Shackleton and his team all returned safely to UK two years after they set out.[1]

On 23 June 2018, 12 members of a youth football team, aged 11 to 16, and their 25-year-old assistant football coach were trapped in a flooded cave network in Thailand. For more than a week, the group had no contact with the outside world. On 2 July, two divers found them four kilometres from the cave entrance, but narrow passageways, rising water and strong currents hampered rescue efforts. More than 10,000 people, including 100 divers, were involved in freeing the boys and their coach, who were eventually rescued between 8 and 10 July.[2]

The need for resilience during and after the pandemic

Resilience is important because it gives us the strength to overcome difficulties and hardships.

The COVID-19 pandemic, which is still prevalent at the time of writing this book, has had a huge impact on everyone's day-to-day lives. It has taken away many of our freedoms and completely changed the way we work and

---

[1] For more information about Shackleton's expedition, visit: *www.rmg.co.uk/stories/topics/sir-ernest-shackleton*.

[2] For more information, visit: *www.bbc.co.uk/news/world-asia-44695232*.

interact with colleagues. It has exposed how fragile we are as human beings.

On a personal level, the pandemic has deprived us of things such as contact with loved ones, socialising, eating out in restaurants, playing contact sports, leisure activities, travelling and holidays. Many have put plans for the future on hold and there is a general feeling that 'normal life' will take a long time to return.

Insecurity at work, financial and health worries, and a lack of control over our lives has led to some people feeling overwhelmed and unable to cope. Being resilient in these difficult circumstances is essential if we are to overcome challenges, remain positive and work through problems.

Even pre-pandemic, the work environment had become one of constant change. People could no longer expect stability in a job. For example, Generation Z (people born 1997 to 2010) are three times more likely to change jobs in the first decade of their working career than baby boomers (people born between 1946 and 1964) did in their first decade at work.[3]

Working time has also become increasingly fluid. The sophistication of technology means that businesses are no longer limited to specific geographical locations to manage their workforce, enabling people to work remotely. The number of people working remotely has risen through

---

[3] *https://blog.linkedin.com/2018/october/11/the-job-hopping-generation-young-professionals-are-on-the-move*.

necessity during the pandemic, with home working an important part of business continuity.

Many experts believe that post COVID-19, the world of work will change further. Offices will still exist but as places of collaboration, idea exchanges and innovation. Working from home will be the norm for most employees most of the time. Office visits will be limited to team meetings, events and check-ins with managers. Indeed, a 2020 Gartner survey revealed that 74% of CFOs and finance business leaders planned to keep their previously on-site workforce working remotely post COVID-19.[4]

Homeworking challenges include isolation and childcare. These issues have been accentuated during lockdown, with people unable to socialise and schools closed, and remain a threat to employee well-being as businesses strive to manage uncertainty.

The impact of the pandemic and the instability and stress this brings, coupled with the knowledge that the world of work will need to change post-COVID-19 to deal with economic uncertainties, means that resilience is now more important than ever.

We need to build our resilience to cope effectively with ambiguity and change and to bounce back in the face of adversity. This is particularly important if we manage and

---

[4] *www.gartner.com/en/newsroom/press-releases/2020-04-03-gartner-cfo-surey-reveals-74-percent-of-organizations-to-shift-some-employees-to-remote-work-permanently2*.

lead others at work. Managers have a critical role in creating a motivating environment where team members want to give their best. How we react as leaders and managers influences others' motivation levels.

Characteristics of resilient work professionals

How do you know when someone is resilient? What are the characteristics that set them apart?

First, it is important to say that resilient people are not perfect. They too struggle, are impacted by stressful situations, make mistakes, and may need to ask for help. However, their attitude and approach enable them to cope and overcome life's challenges.

Resilient people:

- Have an 'internal focus of control'. They recognise what they can control and what they can't. They feel in control of their own destiny – a survivor, not a victim. They recognise that they have a choice in how they react to unfavourable situations.
- Manage their own emotions. They know themselves well and actively manage their own feelings in times of stress.
- Keep calm in times of crisis. They recognise life is full of challenges and they trust in themselves and others to cope and survive.
- Are realistic and solution-orientated. They don't ask why something has happened but instead concentrate

on what they or others can do to resolve it. In other words, they have good problem-solving skills.

- Are open, flexible and able to change their approach according to the circumstances.
- Can motivate themselves to act and at the same time are empathetic to others around them and lead by example.

The good news is that these skills can be built over time.

The link between resilience and well-being – taking care of mental, emotional, social and physical health

Studies show that resilient people are less stressed, less depressed and happier with their lives. To build resilience, we need to take care of our mental, emotional, social and physical, health.

These areas are sometimes called our 'thinking', 'feeling', 'being' and 'doing' energies. What we think, what we feel, how we are and what we do affect our performance and our ability to face and solve problems and pick ourselves up again after difficulties.

Thinking

Feeling

Being

Doing

Figure 1: The four energies

For example, our 'feeling' energy or emotional well-being affects us both mentally and physically, and impacts how we interact with others. For instance, if we feel fearful and anxious, it can make us feel physically unwell and it can restrict our desire to interact with other people.

In the following chapters, I provide tips and actions you can take to improve your resilience by boosting each of your four energies. We'll look at the challenges for managers of building resilience in themselves and their teams, and how to recognise when you need to do this. There is also a self-assessment questionnaire to determine your own levels of resilience and pinpoint where you can develop your skills.

Reflection and action points from this chapter

In preparation for the following chapters, take a moment to consider what prompted you to read this book.

Write a few notes about what you want to change about your mental, emotional, social and physical health. I will ask you to refer back to these objectives later.

CHAPTER 2: THE CHALLENGES FOR MANAGERS OF BUILDING RESILIENCE IN THEMSELVES AND OTHERS

Introduction

In this chapter, we look at how to tell when you actively need to build your resilience and why people find this so difficult, and why increasing your own resilience and that of your team is important.

Case study

Pallia and her partner live together with their two children.

Pallia has been working from home since the first lockdown. Pallia works from a bedroom that has been converted into an office, and her partner, who also works from home, uses the kitchen table.

Pallia manages a team of six people, three of whom have been furloughed. The business she works for is struggling in the difficult economic circumstances. As the pandemic has progressed, Pallia has become increasingly concerned about the long-term viability of her job.

Pallia's partner is in sales and the business he works for has also been impacted. He has had to take a 20% pay cut. In the past, the couple relied on his large annual bonus and sales commissions to help pay their large mortgage, but these have also been cut. As a result, they are struggling financially. Pallia and her partner have already taken a mortgage holiday and now are using their credit cards, which are at their maximum credit limits, to pay for their day-to-day living. Pallia's partner has been applying for other jobs, but the market is saturated, and he feels lucky to at least have his current position.

The couple have been home-schooling their two children, aged six and eight, when the schools have been closed during lockdown. One of the children has learning difficulties and this has put increasing strain on the home environment. Pallia's partner works for an American company and often has calls and meetings late into the evening, which means that he has little time to help with childcare.

Pallia finds herself in a constant state of anxiety. She feels isolated and vulnerable at work and is conscious that two of her team members are not coping well with working from home. She has tried to keep in contact with the people on her team who have been furloughed, but this is increasingly difficult. Her relationship with her boss has always been slightly strained and now they tend to communicate via email rather than videoconferencing or phone. Recently Pallia missed two important deadlines and she feels she is constantly playing catch-up at work.

Pallia juggles childcare each day and feels guilty she is not a better mother or teacher. In addition, she is very concerned about her parents' welfare. She is an only

> child and has not seen her parents for more than six months as they have been self-isolating.
>
> The inability to plan for the future, and the thought that even if all goes well, she and her partner will be in financial difficulties for a long time, leaves Pallia feeling overwhelmed, often on the edge of tears and unable to cope.

Lack of control

Does Pallia's situation sound familiar?

Feeling you lack control and that things are getting out of hand can have a detrimental effect on health and well-being. In the case study, Pallia is certainly stressed, and her current work and home situation is pulling on her reserves of resilience.

We all need a degree of stimulation at work in to be efficient and effective. If we are just sitting twiddling our thumbs, our performance is low. However, if we feel overwhelmed and have too much to do our work performance also diminishes and we can suffer physically and mentally, leading to exhaustion and illness.

2: The challenges for managers of building resilience in themselves and others

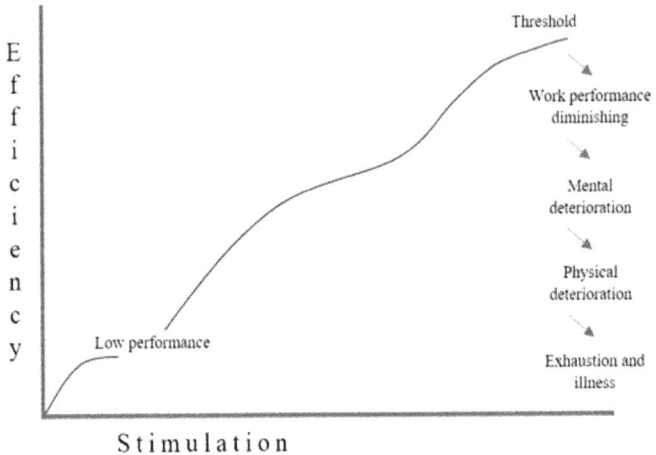

Figure 2: The efficiency threshold

Typical causes of stress

Pre-pandemic, typical causes of stress at work included lack of time, frustrations at work, the pressure of meeting deadlines, relationship breakdowns, change, boredom and bureaucracy. During and post-pandemic, job security and isolation factors may also cause people to feel overwhelmed and unable to cope.

Outside work, we have additional pressures:

- Health worries and illness
- Losing a loved one
- Crisis in relationships
- Family pressures
- Financial worries

- Poor living conditions
- Moving home
- Unemployment
- Caring for others
- Poor self-esteem

If you work remotely, you may not have the support network to help you cope with stress that can exist when you work from one central location on a nine-to-five basis.

When pressure turns to stress: spotting the signs of a decrease in well-being and resilience

As we have seen, some degree of pressure helps work performance. Indeed, there is such a thing as positive stress. Called 'eustress' (the opposite of 'distress'), it helps us to focus our energy and motivates us to achieve our short-term goals. Eustress is the excitement we feel when working up to completing a major, important task. It is when we know we can cope with the pressure; in fact, it improves our performance.

Conversely, distress, which can be short- or long-term, is when we feel we cannot cope. It causes us anxiety or concern, is unpleasant and negatively affects our performance.

When distress occurs, we experience physical, emotional and behavioural effects:

2: The challenges for managers of building resilience in themselves and others

Table 1: Physical Signs of Stress

Pressure	Stress
Good posture	Poor posture
Relaxed breathing	Rapid breathing/tight chest
Aware of body needs	Indigestion/stomach cramps
Vitality	Shoulder and neck pain
Wellness	Headaches
	Dilated pupils
	Sweating/clammy feeling

Table 2: Emotional Signs of Stress

Pressure	Stress
Confident	Anxious
Efficient	Tense
Pleasure	Distress
Good self-image	Poor self-image

Assertive	Unconfident
Able to cope	Swamped
Energised	Depressed

Table 3: Behavioural Signs of Stress

Pressure	Stress
Focused	Poor concentration
Clarity of thought	Confusion
Awareness	Lack of awareness
Effective planning	Poor planning
Decisive	Indecisive
Objectives achieved	Not completing tasks
Clear communication	Ambiguous communication
Time to rest and relax	Lack of time/fatigue

Self-care

To ensure your own well-being, be aware of the common burnout symptoms. Look at the list below and tick any that relate to you in the past month:

Table 4: Burnout Assessment

	✗	✓
Weight loss/gain		
Tense posture		
Trembling		
Increased smoking/cups of coffee		
Pallor/blushing		
Inarticulate speech		
Sighing		
Colds or infections		
Tearful		
Frowning		

Taking unprescribed drugs		
Twitches, tics		
Not sleeping well		
Dropping things		
Forgetting things		
Biting nails, lip or cheek		
Wanting more time to yourself		
Eating too much/too little		
Late for work, long lunch breaks		
Clock watching		
Reduction in output		
Making mistakes		
Having aches and pains		
Losing temper, mood swings, overreacting		

Withdrawing socially		
Failing to meet deadlines		
Feeling sick		
Expecting yourself to do more/better		
Feeling angry, hurt, worried, unhappy		
Having minor accidents		

If you are feeling anxious or depressed, here is a free self-assessment that will point you in the direction of help and support:

www.nhs.uk/conditions/stress-anxiety-depression/mood-self-assessment/.

Coping with stress

If you do find your well-being affected by uncertainty and change and/or you are experiencing any of the burnout symptoms listed above, it is important to act to prevent further decline and illness. At times of stress and when things are not going OK, you actively need to build your resilience. Many people find this difficult as they will not admit even to themselves that things are wrong. They may find it difficult to reach out for help or not know how or what to do to move things forward.

2: The challenges for managers of building resilience in themselves and others

In the following chapters you will find tips on how to boost your resilience. The resilience questionnaire in the next chapter is also a useful diagnostic to help you identify where to focus.

Watch out for signs of stress in others

As well as keeping an eye on your own well-being, your workload and the balance of home and work life, look out for signs of stress in members of your team.

With more people working from home and regular working patterns changing, gone are the days when a quick stop at someone's desk or a chat by the water fountain would give the manager a sense of the state of team morale. As the work climate becomes more difficult and less cohesive, and without face-to-face interaction, it's easy to miss the cues to pinpoint someone's state of mind. It is essential therefore that managers make a sustained effort to tune into the well-being of their team when they are working remotely or when working patterns have changed.

Watch out for mood swings and unusual behaviour in your team members. Keep in regular contact, be supportive and be available to offer a listening ear. It is helpful to discuss how you and others are feeling in team meetings and agree any actions to help improve well-being in the workplace. In chapter 8, I provide tips and ideas for ways you can build resilience in the team.

The consequences if resilience declines for the manager and for the team

You may think that no one notices if the team manager is not feeling at their best – but employees are extremely sensitive to their boss's mood and behaviour.

Consider for a moment how your own boss has reacted to the pandemic and how they have been with you in the past month. It is likely that their behaviour is infectious. If positive, it can boost morale and motivation. If negative, it can cause ripples and stress across the whole team.

A manager and a team who are not resilient will probably dwell on problems, not see the way out of difficulties and become overwhelmed. By practising resilience techniques with your team both as an individual and as a manager, you will be able to adopt a proactive approach to daily life.

Reflection and action points from this chapter

Take five minutes to write down how you are feeling right now and how this is impacting how you interact with your colleagues. Reflect on what this tells you about your current state of well-being and level of happiness.

CHAPTER 3: ASSESS YOUR OWN LEVELS OF RESILIENCE

This chapter provides a resilience self-assessment inventory for you – and your team – to use. It will highlight your areas of strength and help you identify where you can improve your resilience. The following chapters then provide ideas on how you can develop such resilience skills.

Resilience self-assessment inventory

Complete the self-assessment below as honestly as possible. There are no right or wrong answers, so please be honest.

Table 5: Physical Resilience Assessment

	Disagree completely	Strongly disagree	Somewhat disagree	Somewhat agree	Strongly agree	Agree completely
	1	2	3	4	5	6
Physical well-being/'doing'						

3: Assess your own levels of resilience

	Disagree completely	Strongly disagree	Somewhat disagree	Somewhat agree	Strongly agree	Agree completely
	1	**2**	**3**	**4**	**5**	**6**
I undertake 30 minutes of exercise 5 times a week						
I have between seven and eight hours' quality sleep a night						
I take regular breaks away from my desk every day						
I eat five portions of fruit and vegetables each day						

	Disagree completely	Strongly disagree	Somewhat disagree	Somewhat agree	Strongly agree	Agree completely
	1	2	3	4	5	6
I make time every day to relax and clear my mind						
I switch off my phone/commun-ication devices/arrange cover when I am away from work						
Total score						

Table 6: Emotional Resilience Assessment

	Disagree completely	Strongly disagree	Somewhat disagree	Somewhat agree	Strongly agree	Agree completely
	1	**2**	**3**	**4**	**5**	**6**
Emotional well-being/'feeling'						
I have a clear sense of purpose in my life						
I feel valued and appreciated for my contribution						
Work provides me with the fulfilment that I need						
I am happy with the amount of uninterrupted quality time I have with the						

3: Assess your own levels of resilience

	Disagree completely	Strongly disagree	Somewhat disagree	Somewhat agree	Strongly agree	Agree completely
	1	**2**	**3**	**4**	**5**	**6**
people who matter in my life						
I am clear about what brings me joy in my life						
I show my gratitude to others						
Total score						

Table 7: Mental Resilience Assessment

	Disagree completely	Strongly disagree	Somewhat disagree	Somewhat agree	Strongly agree	Agree completely
	1	2	3	4	5	6
Mental well-being/'thinking'						
My thinking is clear and rational						
I see the glass half full rather than half empty						
I can quickly move on when things go wrong						
I recognise my strengths and best qualities						

3: Assess your own levels of resilience

	Disagree completely	Strongly disagree	Somewhat disagree	Somewhat agree	Strongly agree	Agree completely
	1	**2**	**3**	**4**	**5**	**6**
I feel in control of my life						
I regularly take time out to forward plan						
Total score						

Table 8: Social Resilience Assessment

	Disagree completely	Strongly disagree	Somewhat disagree	Somewhat agree	Strongly agree	Agree completely
	1	2	3	4	5	6
Social well-being/'being'						
I feel stimulated and energised by the relationships I have with others						
I feel comfortable asking for what I want						
I recognise my strengths and best qualities						
If needed, I have work colleagues I can call on for support						

	Disagree completely	Strongly disagree	Somewhat disagree	Somewhat agree	Strongly agree	Agree completely
	1	**2**	**3**	**4**	**5**	**6**
I feel comfortable talking to my family and friends and approaching them for help, support and advice						
If ever I needed medical advice, I would approach my GP without hesitation						
Total score						

How to interpret your scores

Total score:			
Physical well-being	Emotional well-being	Mental well-being	Social well-being
…..	…..	…..	…..

My highest score(s): …..

My lowest score(s): …..

My total resilience score (the combination of all four category scores): …..

The questionnaire is designed to assess your total resilience as a whole person. Your relative levels of physical, emotional, mental and social well-being contribute to your overall resilience levels.

Look first at your overall score:

- A score of 120 and above indicates high levels of resilience.
- A score between 95 and 119 indicates average levels of resilience.
- A score between 60 and 94 indicates low levels of resilience.
- A score between 0 and 59 indicates very low levels of resilience.

Next, highlight which of the four categories you scored highest and lowest in.

Table 9: High and Low Scoring Categories

Highest scoring category	Lowest scoring category

The four energies and why they matter

Physical energy

Our physical energy determines our ability to respond positively and proactively when we are challenged, things don't go our way or we are stressed. Living a healthy lifestyle helps our resilience in the following ways:

- Seven to eight hours sleep a night allows us sufficient sleep to recharge our batteries.
- Drinking water throughout the day hydrates us and improves mood and brain function as well as energy levels.
- Eating a balanced diet gives us the right 'fuel' to keep our energy levels high.

- Regular exercise boosts our feel-good factors, lowers blood pressure and counters stress.
- Taking regular breaks away from our desk and switching off from work while on holiday helps us maintain a sense of perspective.

Emotional energy

Knowing and accepting who you are and what you stand for helps build your emotional energy or 'feeling'. Having a sense of purpose helps provide meaning in your life. It also helps us to identify our passions and to stay focused on what is important. We can draw on emotional energy when things go wrong as it helps put things in perspective. People with high levels of emotional well-being know what their core values are. They are clear about what brings them joy in their lives, feel valued and are appreciative of those around them.

Mental energy

Research shows that positive mental energy has a significant impact on both the body and the brain. Positive thinking produces an effect called 'cognitive broadening'.[5] This means the mind broadens its attention and thought patterns when we think positively rather than narrowing

---

[5] Cognitive broadening is a theory developed by Barbara Fredrickson. For more information on the Broaden-and-Build Theory, see *www.ncbi.nlm.nih.gov/pmc/articles/PMC1693418/*.

our attention and restricting thought patterns as happens when we are in a negative mental state.

By adopting a positive mental state, we:

- Can tackle more complex ideas;
- Learn more;
- See opportunities, possibilities and solutions;
- Attract others, so we are less isolated (whereas negative thinkers become more isolated); and
- Have improved health outcomes as cardiovascular function is impacted by positive emotions.

Social energy

Human beings are social creatures by nature. Social isolation can lead to high risks of illness and early death.

People who feel more connected to others:

- Have higher self-esteem;
- Have more empathy for others;
- Are more trusting and cooperative; and
- Have lower levels of anxiety and depression.

Reflection and action points from this chapter

As we come to the end of this chapter, consider what your overall resilience score tells you about where you are right now.

Look at where you scored lowest. Read the relevant chapter for hints and tips on how to improve your resilience over time.

CHAPTER 4: TIPS FOR PHYSICAL WELL-BEING

In this chapter, we look at how physical well-being affects our mental health, how to increase the amount of movement and exercise you do and how sleeping and eating well helps your well-being.

Activity and mood

Physical exercise improves how you feel, how you think and how much energy you have to do things. It is one of the most powerful mood-enhancing activities. Physical activity increases the levels of endorphins (feel-good chemicals) in the brain which are natural mood boosters and help you feel more relaxed. Physical exercise reduces anxiety and depression, boosts energy and brainpower as well as enhancing self-esteem.

Case study

Daniel is an IT manager at a large global services firm.

He has had little time or motivation in the past year to undertake any regular exercise. The past 12 months have been extremely demanding, both from work and personal perspectives.

Like the rest of his colleagues, Daniel has been working remotely for more than a year due to the COVID-19 pandemic. He has been extremely busy with a large project.

In the past year Daniel has also split from his long-term partner, with whom he has a 13-year-old daughter. He is now living in a rented studio flat with very little room to spare.

Daniel used to exercise at a gym near his office three times a week, but as he now rarely goes into the office, he has stopped this routine. He seldom leaves his flat during the week and spends most evenings either working or playing video games. Daniel feels he is a victim of difficult circumstances. He acknowledges he may be depressed and should start exercising again, but it all seems too difficult.

Does this scenario sound familiar?

- "More than a quarter of the world's adult population (1.4 billion adults) are insufficiently active
- Worldwide, around 1 in 3 women and 1 in 4 men do not do enough physical activity to stay healthy
- Insufficient activity increased by 5% (from 31.6% to 36.8%) in high-income countries between 2001 and 2016"[6]

Humans are programmed to move, but as the nature of work has changed over time, we are spending less and less time being physically active. This has long-term consequences. The more we stay 'glued' to our screens, the more difficult it is for us to become active. Inactivity breeds

---

[6] *www.who.int/news-room/fact-sheets/detail/physical-activity*.

inactivity. Furthermore, if you are already feeling stressed or depressed, it is very likely that you lack the motivation to physically move. This lack of movement can lead to a downward spiral of inactivity, poor mental well-being and ill-health.

Building physical activity into your daily routine

Most of us know that physical activity is good for us, but in practice the resolutions we make to increase our levels of fitness often dissipate over time. Other priorities take over or we set ourselves unrealistic objectives that become too challenging or difficult to achieve. We end up feeling demotivated and bad about ourselves as we have not reached our goal.

If you are leading a sedentary lifestyle and currently do little or no exercise, it's useful to identify where to start. Consider the following questions:

- Have you ever exercised before – if so, what did you do and why did you give it up?
- If you have never exercised before, what stopped you?
- What type of exercise appeals to you?
- How important is it that you exercise with others?
- How do you feel about online exercise?
- What is the optimum time of day for you to exercise?
- What one thing could you do tomorrow to start exercising?

Here are some tips to embed exercise into your routine so it does not become an obligation or chore:

- Choose something that you enjoy doing that elevates the heart rate.
- Find easy ways to get more exercise into your day – for example, walk at a faster tempo, take the stairs.
- It is better to 'start small' and set yourself a realistic goal – e.g. five minutes of exercise a day rather than an hour. Completing an hour's workout simply to achieve a goal rather than enjoying it is short-sighted and not sustainable.
- Piggyback your exercise onto any activity you do on a regular basis – for example if you start each morning by making a fresh juice, do a five-minute stretch beforehand. By 'piggybacking' a new activity onto an existing habit, we are more likely to remember to do it.

Remember that activity isn't just about working out or sport – there are other ways you can exercise. Doing the gardening, cleaning or taking the dog for a walk are all ways to stay physically active.

Making plans to do manageable activities helps to get the wheels in motion. The process will get easier as the days and weeks go by.

For example, pre-lockdown, I realised I needed to increase the amount of physical activity I undertook each week, particularly on work days, as I often came home feeling very tired. I started by setting myself the goal of walking for an hour after work one day a week. This seemed (and was) an achievable goal. I found I liked the activity and felt

I could increase my walking after work to twice a week. After three to four weeks, I noticed I was less tired, and this spurred me to walk three days a week. This is manageable for me (I find three days is an achievable goal) and I have kept up this routine even in lockdown. As a result, I've noticed a marked increase in my energy levels.

Eating well

When we eat well, we feel and think better, and we have more energy. How nutritious is your food? Eating regularly and healthily is important:

- Drink water regularly throughout the day. This helps you think clearly, concentrate as well as helping memory. It also has physical benefits such as helping reduce blood pressure.
- Avoid caffeine intake in the afternoons and evening as it disrupts sleep patterns.
- Ensure your diet is rich in healthy whole foods, fruit and vegetables.

One way to help you take control of what you are eating is to keep a food diary. Write down everything you eat and drink over the course of a week, then review what you have consumed.

Consider:

- How were your mood, sleep and energy levels impacted by what you ate?
- What were you happy with regarding your food and drink intake for the week?

- What changes do you want to make to the type of food and drinks you consume?
- What do you need to do to make the changes you want?

Quality sleep

Having between seven and eight hours' sleep each night is important to our well-being. There are many factors that can interfere with a good night's sleep — from work stress to family worries, illnesses, and other unexpected challenges.

While you might not be able to control the factors that interfere with your sleep, you can adopt habits that encourage better sleep. Here are some simple tips:

- Make sure you have between seven and nine hours' sleep each day.
- Go to bed and get up at the same time every day. Your body's sleep–wake cycle is reinforced by a regular sleep pattern. Even on the days you are not working, get up no more than an hour after your normal waking time.
- Ensure the room you sleep in is cool, quiet and dark. Avoid exposure to light, especially screen time, just before bedtime.
- Avoid heavy or large meals, caffeine, alcohol and nicotine within a couple of hours of bedtime.

- Regular physical activity and spending time outside can promote better sleep, but try not to be too active just before you go to bed.
- To promote sleep, do relaxation activities before bedtime, such as taking a bath or using relaxation techniques. Examples include deep breathing, taking three long breaths in and then three long breaths out and starting from your head and moving down the body, visualising relaxing your muscles in each part of the body.
- If you have trouble going to sleep, use simple relaxation techniques. Meditation also can ease anxiety.
- If you wake up in the middle of the night and start to think about things, keep a notepad and pen by the side of your bed and write down what you want to remember without turning the light on.

Take regular breaks

We can only focus for a maximum of 90 minutes before our concentration wanes. Our sedentary lifestyles mean that we need to consciously get up from our desks or the sofa and move and take regular breaks.

- Put a timer on your phone or a reminder on your laptop to take a break after a maximum of 90 minutes.
- Stop and make yourself a drink away from your desk.
- Walk round the block, the garden or even the next room.

- Meet someone you know for a short catch up.
- Meditate for a few minutes.
- Doodle or do something to distract yourself from your screen.

It is important to manage boundaries between work and home, especially if you are working from home, so find ways to switch off such as having a set time limit for finishing work, and putting your laptop and work phone away at night and when you are on holiday. Importantly, turn off your work social media notifications when you finish work and refrain from sending emails, posting on social media or messaging colleagues outside working hours.

Reflection and action points from this chapter

If you had to make an improvement in one of four areas outlined in this chapter (physical activity, eating well, quality sleep and taking regular breaks), which would it be?

Write a paragraph describing what your life would be like if you made this improvement. What would you be doing differently? What would change around you? What would the impact be?

Now consider how you can make these changes – and when and how you will do this.

CHAPTER 5: TIPS FOR EMOTIONAL WELL-BEING

What is emotional well-being?

Leaders such as Mahatma Gandhi and Nelson Mandela embodied high levels of emotional well-being. They radiated a sense of purpose, a clear set of values, and integrity that helped them surmount many difficulties.

Emotional well-being is about how we 'are' with ourselves. Some people see this as the 'spiritual' side of our being, about having a 'soul'. Emotional well-being comes from having a strong understanding of oneself, a sense of meaning and purpose and a set of values and principles that can guide us in our decision-making and how we live our life.

If you your score was low in this area, here are some activities to increase this energy:

Writing your vision

Identifying your purpose and vision is an important step towards personal understanding and acceptance and is a great way of focusing on how you need to be. Planning how to live out your vision will create inner happiness and satisfaction.

To create your personal vision, answer these questions:

1. What do you want most out of life?
2. If you could be exactly the kind of person you wanted, what would your qualities be?

3. What is your ideal professional or vocational situation? What impact would you like your efforts to have?
4. What material things are important for you to own?
5. What would you like to create in the arena of individual learning, travel, reading or any other activities that are important to you?
6. What is your ideal living environment?
7. What do you want to see happen in the world?
8. What is your desire for health, fitness, athletics and anything to do with your body?
9. What type of relationships would you like to have with friends, family and others?
10. What else, in any other area of your life, would you like to create?
11. Imagine that your life has a unique purpose – fulfilled through what you do, your interrelationships, and the way you live. How would you describe that purpose?

Read through your answers and then formulate a purpose:

My purpose in life is to ....

If you are a visual person, you may wish to represent your vision/purpose pictorially and draw it on a piece of paper.

When you have created your vision, ask yourself if this is what you want. If the answer is yes, how you will ensure that your purpose is fulfilled?

If the answer is no, go back through the questions and identify where the lack of alignment is until you have a purpose that you are happy with.

Identifying your personal values

Identifying what's personally of value to you and that you hold dear is a useful exercise in self-understanding.

The list below gives a wide range of values that may help you pinpoint what is important to you. Feel free to add any other values you may think of. Then, tick the things that are most important to you. Look to highlight up to eight key values.

Accuracy	Achievement	Adventure
Challenge	Change	Competence
Competing with others	Contact with others	Cooperating with others
Creativity	Democracy	Development
Ecology	Effectiveness	Excellence
Excitement	Expertise	Fame
Fast pace	Flexible working hours	Freedom
Friendships	Having a family	Helping people

Honesty	Independence	Influence
Integrity	Involvement	Job location
Knowledge	Lack of pressure	Leadership
Love	Loyalty	Making decisions
Managing others	Meaningful work	Money
Openness	Order	Personal development
Physical challenge	Power	Pressure
Privacy	Promotion	Recognition
Relationships	Reputation	Responsibility
Routine	Security	Sense of community
Serenity	Stability	Status
Taking risks	The environment	Tranquillity
Truth	Variety	Wisdom

Working alone	Working well with colleagues	Working with people outside the organisation

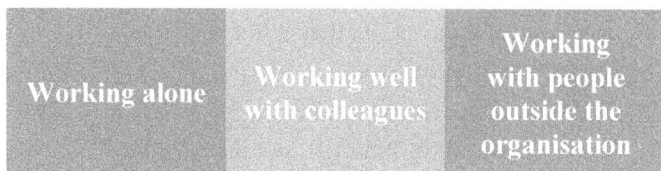

Select your top eight priorities from the list above and detail what they mean to you. This will help you to identify and measure when these values are being met.

1. _____

2. _____

3. _____

4. _____

5. _____

6. _____

7. _____

8. _____

Consider:

- Which values do not complement your purpose (vision)? If so, what if any, do you need to change?
- How closely do your personal life and the organisation you are working in fulfil these values?

- How important is it that your personal life and organisation reflect these values?
- What do you want to do if either your personal life or the organisation is not fulfilling these values?

By gaining clarity on your own purpose and values, you will be in a position to remain congruent in what you believe, do and say. It will help you base your decisions on a deeper self-knowledge.

What is important to you?

In this section we look at the activities you like to do best and which are important to you, on the basis that doing things you love makes you more resilient to stress.

1. Identify something you are passionate about, aspire to or dream of achieving. What have you done to realise this, why have you not achieved it, and how are you going to if you want to?

2. Over three days, write down your answer to the question "What is important to me?" Afterwards, ask yourself "Is how I spend my time reflective of what is important to me?"

3. List the people in your life who matter to you most. Give a rating on a scale of 1 (low) to 10 (high) for the quality time you have with them. Consider how you can increase these scores.

4. What three things will you do over the next month to increase the levels of happiness you can create for yourself and others?

5: Tips for emotional well-being

Do things that make you feel fulfilled

Here are two suggestions for activities that can make you feel more fulfilled in life.

How are you spending your time?

This activity is designed to help you assess and realign what is important to you in your life and how you are spending your time.

- First, list the things that are most important in your life – the things that bring you joy.
- Keep a diary over the week so you can record at 30-minute intervals how you are spending your time.
- Analyse the results of your calendar activity. Consider where you spend the most of your time and whether you are happy about this. How much time do you spend on activities that bring you joy and fulfilment? What can you do to rectify this balance?

Be kind

Feed your soul and do a random act of kindness. If you make someone else happy, it makes you happy.

- Pay for someone's bus ticket – you don't have to know them.
- Bake a cake and deliver it to a neighbour.
- Fill your partner's car up with petrol.
- Pay the toll for the car behind you.
- Give up an hour of your time to volunteer for a cause that is dear to you.

As an example, during the COVID-19 pandemic I discovered that in my neighbourhood, there is a 90-year-old lady who lives by herself and has no family. As she was self-isolating, I offered to do her shopping and bring her a hot meal at the weekend. Although I can't go into her house, I really look forward to my encounters with her and we have developed a mutually rewarding friendship.

Reflection and action points from this chapter

You may find it strange to consider emotional well-being. However, studies show that taking care of your soul and being can help strengthen your sense of self and your ability to be resilient.

Challenge yourself to undertake one of the activities from this chapter.

CHAPTER 6: TIPS FOR MENTAL WELL-BEING

The power of the mind

Resilient people have been shown to have good mental health and an internal 'locus of control'. They believe that events in life (good and bad) are largely caused by controllable factors like attitude, preparation and hard work, and hold themselves accountable for making changes. In this chapter, I provide tips and tools to encourage the development of a positive mental outlook. I also signpost sources of help if you or your team are suffering from poor mental health.

Positive thinking

To act positively, we need to first think that way. Often our ability to be proactive is prohibited by our limiting beliefs – "I can't…"; "I mustn't…"; "I should…".

If the 'self-talk' in our head is negative, it can affect our ability to face adversity and bounce back.

Use the activity below to identify the negative beliefs and/or thoughts going on in your head, before turning them into something positive and productive.

Table 10: Activity

What negative beliefs do you hold about yourself? What are you telling yourself in your head?	How do these beliefs make you feel?	Who/where are those thoughts coming from? What evidence do you have that this is true about you?
E.g. "I can't express my concerns to my boss", "I'm not worth bothering about."	*E.g. "Anxious, fearful."*	*E.g. "Being teased at school", "Being overlooked for promotion at work."*

What do you need to believe and tell yourself to make you feel and act positively?

E.g. "I can talk openly about my issues to my boss", "My concerns are valid and worthwhile."

Other ways to increase your ability to think positively are:

- Be more conscious of your self-talk throughout the day. What are you telling yourself – is it positive or negative?
- Practise positive self-talk. Don't say anything to yourself that you wouldn't say to someone else.
- Develop your assertiveness skills to help you communicate your needs, wants and expectations.
- Avoid negative people. Start conversations with people who are positive, as positivity rubs off.
- Watch a comedy film, read a funny book or share a joke. Laugh more often. Laughter triggers the release of endorphins, the body's natural feel-good chemical, which decreases stress.

Recognise your strengths

If you don't believe in yourself, it's difficult to get other people to believe in you. People who are resilient recognise their own achievements; they can draw on their strengths when times are challenging.

Make a list of your achievements and things you are proud of. Keep a success diary on your calendar so that at the end of each day you can list what has gone well and what you are pleased about. Focusing on positives helps make us more optimistic about life.

Answer the following questions:

- What is the best thing about you?
- What do you like most about yourself?
- What do you enjoy doing most?
- What brings out your best?
- What is your most significant achievement?
- What makes you feel you are being who you really are?
- What are you most looking forward to in the future?
- How can your strengths help you in the future?

Circles of influence and control

Management guru Stephen Covey says: "Resilient people spend time expanding their circle of influence, instead of becoming trapped in their circle of concern." In his book

The Seven Habits of Highly Effective People[7], Covey introduces the concept of circles of concern, influence and control. He explains resilient people spend their time and energy focusing on situations and events that they have control over and do not spend time worrying about things that they cannot change or control.

- The circle of concern is the area that we have no control over.
- The circle of influence is the area that we have influence over.
- The circle of control is the area we have direct control over.

The circle of concern is where we tend to focus, but it depletes our energy as we have no control over events in this area. We can only react. For example, we can't control the economy or an organisational restructure. The energy focused on the circle of concern is negative.

Proactive people focus on the circles of influence and control. The circle of control is the area we have control over and where we can act in a positive manner. For example, we can control what and when we eat or how we respond to an email. The circle of influence represents things outside our direct control but over which you have influence. For example, you may be able to influence your

---

[7] *The 7 Habits of Highly Effective People: Powerful Lessons in Personal Change* by Stephen R. Covey, Free Press, New York, 2004.

manager about an upcoming decision at work or your partner about the choice of restaurant.

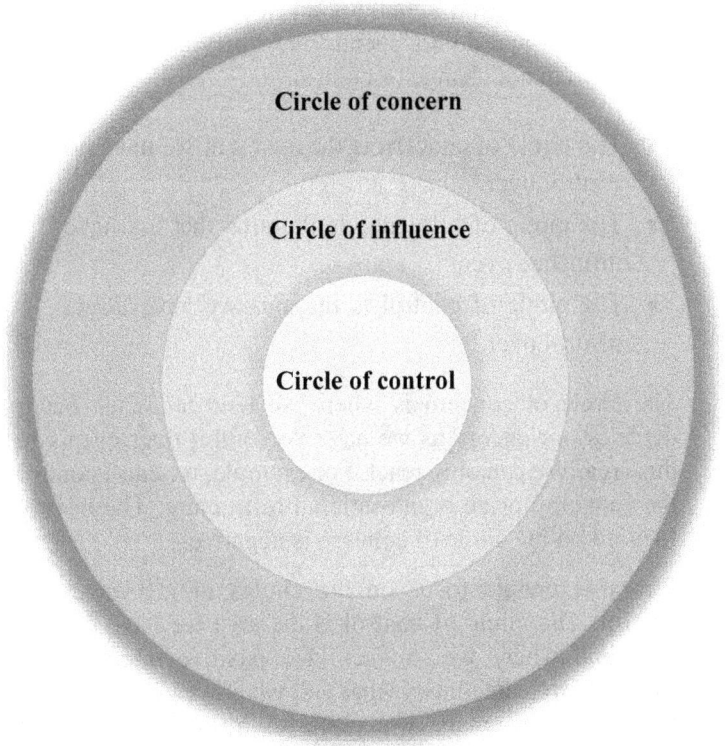

Circle of concern

Circle of influence

Circle of control

Figure 3: Circles of concern, influence and control

If you focus on the circle of concern and neglect the circles of influence and control, eventually these two circles will get smaller. This will add to feelings of stress and helplessness because you cannot change anything in the circle of concern. You become a victim of circumstance rather than a survivor.

When you act on your circle of influence and within your circle of control, you can reduce stress levels and increase happiness, because you can initiate and influence change.

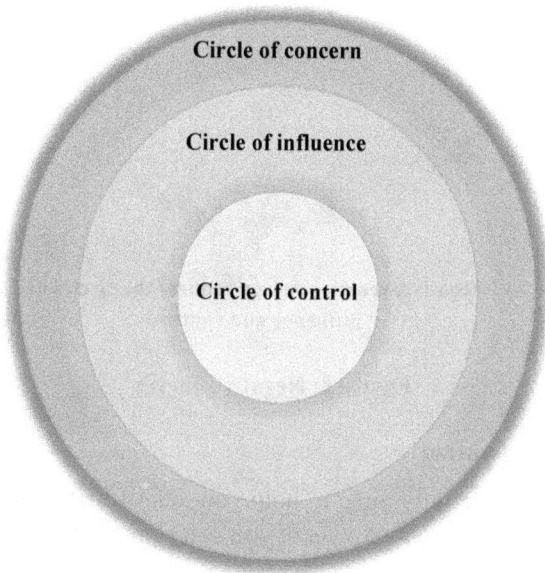

Circle of concern

Circle of influence

Circle of control

Positive, reactive energy enlarges the circles of influence and control

Figure 4: Positive energy

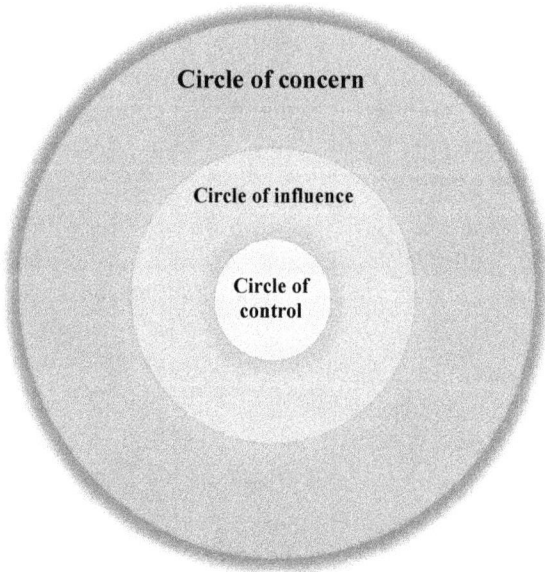

Negative, reactive energy reduces the circles of
influence and control

Figure 5: Negative energy

Taking control

This next activity aims to help you identify when you are
feeling overwhelmed, where you can be more in control.

Step 1:

Make a list of things on your mind right now – what you
are thinking about, worrying about, working on?

What I'm anxious about today is ...

Step 2:

Draw three circles:

1. Areas I can control
2. Areas I can influence
3. Areas of concern

Work through each item on your list and decide if it is something you can control or influence. If it is, put it in the appropriate circle. If it's not, put it in your circle of concern.

Step 3:

Now look at the areas you can control. Identify what actions you can take to focus your energy and effort in a proactive way.

- *One thing I can do in a proactive way is ...*
- *How I can prepare for this is ...*

Next, look at the areas that you can influence and identify what you can proactively do and prepare.

Step 4:

Draw on your positive resources. Write down the answer to the statement:

The resources I have to help me take these actions are ....

This activity helped me personally at a time when I was under a lot of pressure at work and a close relative was very ill in hospital. I felt paralysed with worry. The exercise helped me to establish what I could proactively control and influence and helped me feel less overwhelmed.

Self-coaching questions

If you are struggling with a specific concern or worry, the following self-coaching activity can help. Answering the questions will give you insights into how to overcome your problem.

There are no right or wrong answers. If you can't answer a question, skip to the next one. Or ask yourself: What question should I be asking myself here?

The purpose of the exercise is to help you reflect on potential strategies to overcome the concern or worry and to identify action(s) to help you going forward.

Aim

- What would you like to achieve? (Make sure your goal is achievable. If not, break it down into achievable objectives.)
- Specifically, what would you like to be different?
- By when do you want to see a change? (Ensure this is a realistic time frame.)

Situation

- What is happening right now?
- On a scale of 1 to 10, how much of an issue is it?
- How is it impacting you? In what ways?

- Who else is involved and what is their opinion of the situation?
- What else is relevant?

Experience

- What have you already tried to tackle the issue?
- What experience do you have of similar situations and how have you tackled them in the past?
- What lessons have you learned about navigating tough times?
- What have you seen others do in similar situations?

Strengths

- What strengths do you have to help you overcome the problem?
- What qualities do others admire in you that you could use?

Resources

- Who or what can you turn to for guidance and support?
- What or who can inspire or nourish you?

Options

- What strategies could you adopt to tackle the situation?
- What other ideas and perspectives are there?

- If you were being the best you could be, what would your instinct tell you to do?
- What other ideas can you brainstorm, no matter how silly?

The way forward

- What different perspectives have you gained from this exercise?
- What specific actions can you now take?
- When and how will you take them?
- Who do you need to inform and when will you do this?
- What support do you need?
- How and when will you get that support?

For the last two stages, I suggest writing down your answers. Writing helps you clear your mind and process your emotions.

Breathing techniques

In addition to the 'thinking' exercises listed above, another method of calming the mind is deep breathing. This is a mindful practice that helps reduce stress, slow the heartbeat and reduce blood pressure. Here are three techniques to try:

Tibetan yoga breathing:

Sit comfortably with your spine tall (use a cushion or chair if necessary). Connect with your breath and slow down your breathing. Raise your right arm up as you inhale through both nostrils. As you exhale, block the right nostril and breathe out through the left. On your next inhale, raise your left arm up and when you exhale block the left nostril and breathe out through the right nostril (this completes a full round).

Continue like this for 6–12 rounds.

Deep breathing:

Put your hands on your stomach, fingers spread and just touching. Breathe deeply. If your breath is coming from your diaphragm, you are likely to see your fingers move apart as your breath goes in and out. Breathe deeply for five inhales and exhales.

4/4/4 breath:

Breathe in for a count of four, hold for a count of four and exhale for a count of four.

Repeat for four deep breaths.

Meditation

Meditation is a proven way of stilling the body and the mind. It can be useful in our busy lives. You can practice meditation for as little as five minutes a day and you can do it anywhere. If you're not sure how or where to start, there are apps that can guide you. There are many types of meditation. For example, mindfulness – the awareness of 'something' – is a form of meditation. There are many good books[8] and apps[9] on the topic.

To learn meditation, you can train face to face or online. Like any habit, meditation takes practice, so don't be put off if you don't see instant success. It typically takes around eight weeks of mindfulness-based interventions to be able to meditate effectively and feel the benefits.

Meditation exercises are designed to heighten awareness and appreciation of simple daily tasks and the results they achieve.

Here are two examples of meditation activities:

1. **Everyday action**
   - Think of an everyday action that you take for granted, for example opening a door or starting your laptop. Stop for a moment and consider the action: where you are, what you are about to do, how you feel. What thoughts does this prompt in you? What are you aware of?
   - Instead of going through daily motions on autopilot, take moments to stop and cultivate purposeful awareness of what you are doing

---

[8] *Mindfulness: A Practical Guide to Finding Peace in a Frantic World*, Mark Williams and Dr Danny Penman, Little, Brown Book Group, London, 2011.

[9] Headspace meditation app: *www.headspace.com/headspace-meditation-app*.

and appreciate what these actions bring to your life.

2. **Everyday things**
   - The point of this exercise is to simply appreciate the seemingly insignificant things in life, the things that support our existence but rarely get a second thought amidst our desire for bigger and better things. For example, electricity powers your kettle, the tap provides you with water, your clothes provide warmth.

Identify two things that are insignificant in your life. Consider:

- Have you ever stopped to notice their finer, more intricate details?
- Do you know how these things really work?
- Have you ever thought about what life might be like without these things?
- Have you ever sat down and thought about the relationships between these things?

Find out everything you can about their creation and purpose to truly appreciate the ways in which they support your life.

Be aware when resilience is not helpful

There may be situations at work when individuals believe they should be resilient and cope with a situation, regardless of what it is. This can lead to a feeling of being mentally 'weak' if you cannot cope. If you are working in a toxic work environment, it is important that you speak out and seek advice and support. For example, you can consult your HR department or refer to your organisation's freedom to speak up and whistleblowing policies.

Supporting our mental health

The COVID-19 pandemic, increased isolation and uncertainty have led to a rise in incidents of poor mental health. If you are suffering from a decline in mental well-being, it is important that you seek professional help.

Charities such as Mind UK offer information and support.[10] Your employer may also have an employee assistance scheme. I also provide a list of additional resources for help and support in the acknowledgement page of this book.

Reflection and action points from this chapter

Our mental well-being is precious. Thinking clearly helps us to be calm and proactive under pressure.

The techniques in this chapter are proven to help you boost positivity and to feel more in control. Take time to consider which activities would be useful to you and your team.

---

[10] *www.mind.org.uk/information-support*.

CHAPTER 7: TIPS FOR SOCIAL WELL-BEING

Why social well-being is important

Human beings are by nature social beings. We have a strong in-built desire to connect to others. We develop this need from birth – babies and young children need love and security to survive and thrive. To be lonely is stressful. Some say that this stems from our hunter/gatherer forbearers who needed to group together to avoid attack.[11] Social isolation, on the other hand, is on par with high blood pressure, obesity and lack of exercise as a risk factor for illness and early death.[12]

People who feel more connected to others have been shown to have lower levels of anxiety and depression. In addition, they have higher self-esteem, greater empathy for others, are more trusting and cooperative and, therefore, others are more open to trusting and cooperating with them.

As they work from home and have less day-to-day contact with others, people are feeling increasingly isolated. The

---

[11] *Hunter-Gatherers, Archaeological and Evolutionary Theory*, Second edition, Robert L. Bettinger, Raven Garvey, Shannon Tushingham, Springer Publishing, New York, 2015.

[12] *https://science.sciencemag.org/content/241/4865/540*.

challenge is to create real social connections in a world dominated by technology.

Here are a number of activities, hints and tips that can help you improve your social well-being.

Support network map

To improve your social interactions, start by completing a support network map. This will help you identify who is in your network and the quality of your relationships.

To do this, brainstorm the people who form your network:

- At work
- Other professional organisations
- Family
- Friends
- Health professionals
- Other support networks

For each person, rate whether there is:

1. A strong existing relationship;
2. A relationship you'd like to develop further; or
3. No relationship as you have yet to establish contact.

If you have some missing connections, talk to the people you trust and ask them for their recommendations.

Consider what you can do to improve the quality and/or the quantity of your social interactions.

Connecting with others in a virtual world

You may think that loneliness can be cured via physical contact. One study shows that it is shared experience rather than physical contact that is more important.[13] Here are some suggestions for how to connect with others:

- Make time in your diary to meet up (virtually or in person) and talk openly to the people you value and trust at work.

- At the start of meetings, instead of diving into business, begin with a personal connection, for example a check-in question about a childhood memory or asking participants to choose a picture of a weather condition to illustrate how they are feeling. This can be fun and lighten the mood, and gives everyone a chance to connect and get to know one another on a personal level.

- Be genuinely interested in others. For example, enquire about a person's family (e.g. birthday, pets, health, etc.), ask about an event the person recently experienced or comment on something newsworthy – "What did you think about…?"

- Offer to host virtual team events or to find ways of engendering team spirit. Holding a pub quiz or organising a lunchtime cookery challenge helps

---

[13] *www.ericaboothby.com/what-happens-when-people-attend-to-the-same-thing*.

increase a feeling of shared experience and camaraderie.

- Outside work, consider what hobbies, interests, sports or activities you pursue with others. You might need to join an online group to do this. For example, you may not be able to go to a local gym, but there could be online classes. You may not be able to visit an art gallery, but you can join an art appreciation group and do online visits to national galleries.

- Consider connecting to local interest groups via social media, such as neighbourhood groups that have been formed online.

- When you can meet people either online or in person, smile. People are more likely to smile back and engage with you.

- Keep a diary or write a letter to a friend. If you are not able to connect online or face to face, record your thoughts the old-fashioned way – on paper.

Be grateful

Research shows that people who express their gratitude of others feel more positive about themselves and their lives, and are better able to build strong relationships. They live healthier lives and are more likely to bounce back when difficulty hits. Gratitude is a way of acknowledging the goodness in your life.

Here are some suggestions for expressing gratitude:

- When you wake up each morning for the next week, before doing anything, express to yourself what you are grateful for/why you are blessed.
- Write a thank you note, email or text – this not only makes the other person feel good but also will make you feel better. No time to write? Tell them in person how much you appreciate what they have done for you.
- Count your blessings – set yourself time each day or once a week to write down three things that have gone well for you and that you are grateful for. In doing so, re-live the sensations you experienced connected to the event and the impact it had on you.

As part of my personal development in well-being, I set myself a goal of expressing gratitude. I realised I had never directly expressed my gratitude to my family for the happiness and support they give me. Over the course of two or three months, I made a point of showing my gratitude to them. To my surprise, family members have since expressed their gratitude to me. This has strengthened our relationship and given all those involved, including myself, a 'feel-good' factor.

The power of helping others

Helping others has a powerful impact on our well-being. By helping others, such as via volunteering, you are also helping yourself to feel good and increase your social well-being. The act of giving back to the community boosts your own happiness. In studies, volunteers who gave to others in whatever form on a regular basis showed an improved ability to manage stress and stave off disease, as well as reduced rates of depression and an increased sense of life satisfaction.

Some years ago, during a particularly stressful period at work, I decided to join a voluntary organisation that provides services to the local community. Volunteering added a completely new dimension to my life and put the problems I was facing at work into perspective. I still volunteer for the same organisation today and gain a sense of purpose and fulfilment from helping others, which I believe makes me better able to cope with life's pressures.

Consider how you could provide a helping hand to others, for example a neighbour, an elderly person, a school, a youth club. There are lots of opportunities to volunteer online if physical contact is difficult.

At work, you could volunteer to be a mentor or a coach, for example, or to buddy with someone new to a role.

Reflection and action points from this chapter

Isolation and lack of meaningful human relationships is life-shortening. We are not an island and we need social interaction to live long and healthy lives. This means making a concerted effort to stay in touch with co-workers, family and friends. As we have seen, helping others and showing appreciation can also have a health-boosting effect. Consider what affirming actions you can take to increase the quality of your social interactions.

CHAPTER 8: BUILDING RESILIENCE IN TEAM MEMBERS

Put well-being on the team agenda

In this chapter, we consider the importance of creating a healthy work environment and provide advice on how to do this.

To help build resilience, managers need to make a conscious effort to raise awareness of the need for well-being and resilience in the team and to continually communicate its importance.

This task is more difficult if the manager and the team are working remotely. The manager needs to prioritise regular communication with team members. For example, there could be increased one-to-ones and check-ins to see how things are going with individual team members both on a work and a personal level.

Each team member may have different preferences for the frequency and type of contact you have with them. Ask your team members how they would like to keep you up to date and to communicate with you.

Actions the manager can take to build team resilience

The manager can help the team build its resilience by:

- **Setting expectations** – being clear about roles and responsibilities, standards expected, objectives, deliverables and how these will be measured and monitored;

- **Developing a team charter** – setting ground rules with the team for how they will work together when everyone is not in the office all the time and having regular check-ins with the team about how things are going;

- **Organising training** – providing development opportunities for the team to increase their competence and confidence both in terms of skills and knowledge; and

- **Thanking the team and individual team members** – showing appreciation and highlighting achievements.

Regular two-way communication

When a team works at different times and is geographically dispersed, communication and spontaneous, informal discussion and creativity can suffer. Remote workers who never come into the office miss out on necessary connections and can be some of the least engaged employees.

Technology such as Skype, Messenger, WhatsApp and Microsoft Teams can facilitate communication and collaboration. For example, you can check in with team members each morning via a quick message on Messenger.

Technology can help support virtual team meetings. However, in my experience this should supplement but not replace regular face-to-face meetings and spending time keeping people up to date. Regular team meetings are essential to create a sense of team cohesion.

As well as holding face-to-face team meetings where possible, ensure that one-to-ones with team members allow for physical contact as well as virtual.

Build the social element of work

People can feel isolated when they do not have regular contact with co-workers. The problem when people are in lockdown or geographically dispersed is that they miss the 'coffee machine' conversations and the chance to go to lunch with colleagues. Many people's motivation to come to work involves social interaction.

When staff work remotely, managers should take steps to encourage informal conversations, talking about things other than work. Start a conversation for the sake of it and use icebreakers in team meetings to help people share life experiences. For example, ask people to say what their first pet was or their greatest achievement or their favourite holiday destination. By spending time on people, rather than tasks, managers can help build trust and confidence in the team.

It is also important to stay connected. Use informal communication tools like Messenger and WhatsApp to maintain the social element of work. However, as mentioned earlier, respect the boundaries between work and home life; don't message or email outside office hours, or look at your work messages. It is helpful to establish with the team a communications charter where you agree email and social media etiquette, so everyone is aware of and agrees to the same set boundaries.

If you are holding a face-to-face monthly meeting, you could, for example, ask the team to bring in lunch to share afterwards. Invite people in the team to run a biannual optional social event. Hold away days with the team that include an element of fun and team interaction.

Encourage the team to share and collaborate around work and non-work topics. For example, they can tweet or post on Facebook images of team lunches, off-site events, conferences, evenings out and other fun or collaborative experiences. This helps people feel connected to the team.

My own team has a virtual 'Fun Friday' lunch every month. A different person organises the session each time. They host the virtual lunch and select a theme for the hour. The only constraint is that they must involve everyone where possible and make it fun. Our sessions have included a wide range of activities, from magic to a Mexican-themed lunch. The spirit of the hour is focused on strengthening social interaction among the team.

However, a personal learning is that not everyone in a team may want to engage in this type of social activity – and this is OK. It is helpful therefore to give people permission not to engage in work social activities as they may prefer to fulfil this need outside of the workplace.

The power of recognition

Acknowledge birthdays. People will appreciate that you took the time to get to know them on a deeper level and show appreciation for something other than submitting a project on time.

Recognise achievement and acknowledge someone specifically by name. Give them public praise for a job well done. Share team triumphs and successes.

Career development

Development is a powerful motivator, and most people want to be experts in what they do. Career progression can take many forms: deepening an existing skill set or learning a new skill for example, moving sideways in an organisation to another role of a similar status, undertaking an assignment or a project, moving to a higher-grade post.

Employees who choose to work remotely and have flexible working arrangements should still enjoy career progression. Managers need to be conscious not to be biased in favour of those people who are more physically present in the office. It is important to be fair and create personal development plans for all team members. There should not be a hierarchy of entitlement; everyone should have the opportunity to develop based on merit.

Highlight the importance of well-being

Pay particular attention to your team's stress levels, especially in times of change and uncertainty and if you have remote workers on your team. Isolation can aggravate a period of stress that may be alleviated easily with prompt support.

As a manager, watch out for signs such as a dip in performance – team members missing deadlines, producing poor-quality work and not reaching targets. Monitor the times of day that emails are being sent. Team members may work longer hours than contracted when they are under pressure or work remotely, and this can lead to stress and burnout.

Here is a list of tips and techniques you can use as a manager to help promote well-being:

- Arrange regular face-to-face meetings with team members – don't just rely on teleconferencing or videoconferencing. Seeing each other in person allows you to pick up on signs of excess pressure and stress, and can build closer bonds.
- If you do schedule catch-ups via phone, watch out for the other person's tone of voice and be aware of the impact your tone of voice can have on others.
- Encourage your team to undertake a workstation assessment when they work from home to check it is fit for purpose.
- Discuss with team members how they create work routines and set boundaries when working from home.
- Encourage the team to assess their own stress levels on a regular basis and talk about any issues as they arise.
- Ask each person what they would like most support with now.
- Include a well-being session in a team meeting and share tips about how to maintain a good work-life

balance and techniques for switching off. (You can use some of the activities in this book to help.)

- If you see that someone is struggling, act quickly to offer support.
- Listen, show empathy and understanding, and explore practical solutions with the team member.
- Make sure your team know about any assistance available to them if they are feeling stressed, such as well-being training or employee assistance schemes.
- Ensure the team know that they have another outlet to discuss their issues/worries if they don't want to speak to the manager in this case: HR, other teams?

Team temperature checks

Remember to check in with your team to see how they are feeling as well as what they are doing.

As a consultant, I often work with teams to help facilitate a dialogue around resilience and well-being. Below is a short questionnaire I use to gauge levels of well-being and team morale. This can be completed anonymously by each team member. You then discuss the range of scores and agree resulting improvement actions.

It is useful to use the same team temperature check over time to see what progress, if any, is being made. For example, I facilitated a series of quarterly team meetings over a year with one team in a government department that was undergoing major structural change. The temperature check was a useful way to evaluate the well-being of the team as things changed.

Table 11: Temperature Check

Temperature check	
Please rate on a scale of 1 (low) to 10 (high) your:	**Score**
Satisfaction with the current working arrangements	
Current perception of how well we operate as a team	
Current personal level of morale	
Current level of personal well-being at work	

Discuss the temperature check results with the team so you can understand their perceptions. You can then develop a plan of action, repeat the temperature check at intervals and evaluate progress over time.

One-to-one check-ins around well-being

One-to-one discussions with individual team members gives the manager the opportunity to talk about the individual's general well-being and happiness at work. Ask questions like:

- How are they finding work?
- What is working well for them?
- What barriers are they encountering?

- What do they think about the quality of team interventions?
- How happy are they about the level of communication they receive?

Also pay attention to what is not being said. Check your understanding of the situation and don't make assumptions. For example, you may say: "I sense from what you've described that you're finding it difficult to establish boundaries for stopping working in the evenings at home." The team member may say: "No it isn't that - it's the isolation factors that get me down." Either way, you will have identified the causes of anxiety or stress and you can then help the team member consider how to overcome them.

Team resilience questionnaire

If the team is facing difficulties, challenges or uncertainties, it is helpful to discuss the topic of resilience with them and collectively agree how they can pull together to come through hard times.

Here is a questionnaire you can use with your team to help identify and discuss their perceptions on the level of resilience in the team. Each member of the team scores the questions. The manager then facilitates a discussion around the scores with a view to seeing where there is agreement and the reasons for differences in perspectives, as well as ideas for improvement.

The outcome is the creation of a collectively owned plan of action to help build resilience across the team.

Table 12: Team Resilience Assessment

	Disagree completely	Strongly disagree	Somewhat disagree	Somewhat agree	Strongly agree	Agree completely
	1	2	3	4	5	6
Purpose: The team has a clear purpose that provides direction for working through difficulties.						
Skills and experience: The team has the skills and experience to deal effectively with what is happening.						

	Disagree completely	Strongly disagree	Somewhat disagree	Somewhat agree	Strongly agree	Agree completely
	1	2	3	4	5	6
Trust: There are high levels of trust in the team and a belief that we can rely on each other in times of stress.						
Resources: The team has sufficient resources to manage the difficulties we face.						
Adaptability: The team has the will and the						

	Disagree completely	Strongly disagree	Somewhat disagree	Somewhat agree	Strongly agree	Agree completely
	1	**2**	**3**	**4**	**5**	**6**
ability to adapt to change as necessary.						
Support: We are supportive of each other as a team.						
Positive attitude: We have a positive attitude as a team about finding solutions to the challenges we face.						

	Disagree completely	Strongly disagree	Somewhat disagree	Somewhat agree	Strongly agree	Agree completely
	1	2	3	4	5	6
Influence: The team believes it has the power to influence events that are in its control.						

Case study

An IT team in a national charity faced unprecedented challenges during the pandemic as the organisation experienced a massive drop in revenue. The charity had initially adapted to the changing circumstances by furloughing some workers and asking others to work from home. It then reluctantly decided to ask for some voluntary redundancies as it recognised that it would take some time to recover.

The IT team was not included in the redundancy programme, and its five members are working from home. There has been increased demand for IT interventions and the team is working long hours to install and fix new technology. As well as the additional pressure this involves, the team feels very concerned about its long-term future and whether there will be further redundancies or job furloughs.

The team manager noticed the drop in morale. Some team members were displaying signs of irritability and others were withdrawing into themselves. The manager decided to hold a team meeting around well-being and resilience, which I facilitated as an external consultant. I asked each team member to complete the resilience team questionnaire beforehand.

It emerged from the questionnaires and subsequent discussions that the team felt positive that they:

- Had a sense of purpose;
- Trusted each other;
- Had the skills, experience and resources to do the job; and
- Had the will and ability to adapt to change.

These results were encouraging and boosted team morale.

The discussions also revealed areas of improvement:

- Belief in the team's ability to influence events in its control.
- Having a positive attitude to finding solutions to challenges.

> - Being supportive of each other during difficult times.
>
> The results led to open discussion among team members about the support they needed from their manager and each other. I also facilitated a discussion around what was in the team's control and influence and what was not, and ran an activity with the team around the importance of a positive mindset.
>
> This led to the team creating a plan of action to help improve their resilience levels and well-being. The plan is being regularly reviewed and the manager has made well-being a topic for discussion in all her one-to-ones. The results to date are that, although the organisation is still in difficulty, the team feels more able to cope and deal with challenges.

Compassionate leadership

To create the right conditions for people to be able to express how they are feeling and to seek help where needed, managers need to demonstrate what is called "compassionate" leadership. Compassion is now recognised as an important asset to support employee well-being.[14] Showing compassion can be a great support to employees, particularly when they are feeling vulnerable and overwhelmed.

---

[14] *www.weforum.org/agenda/2021/01/6-global-employers-on-how-to-improve-workplace-mental-health/*.

Far removed from the traditional 'command and control' style of leadership, compassionate leadership means actively listening to team members. It is about arriving at a shared understanding of the challenges they face, empathising and caring for team members and taking action to support and help them.

Reflection and action points from this chapter

If you are a manager, I hope that this chapter has made you consider the amount of time and effort you place on enhancing team members' well-being.

As a manager, you have a duty of care to your team to help create the best working environment for them where they can give their best. Your actions serve as a beacon to employees and by taking time to focus on building resilience in your team, you and the team will be better able to face and overcome difficult situations.

CHAPTER 9: CONCLUSION AND MAKING HABITS STICK

The benefits of building resilience

I hope that this book has convinced you of the benefits of building resilience and how this impacts our physical, emotional, mental and social well-being. The practical tips, activities and advice I have provided should help you to develop your well-being in each of these four areas. This in turn will help increase your resilience and your ability to bounce back.

Review your objectives and set goals

In chapter 1, I asked you to identify what you wanted to gain from this book. I invite you to review your aim and then to list the tips and actions you can take forward after reading this book.

Prioritise any thoughts you have on the actions you can take that will help you increase your resilience. Write your top three actions in the box below:

Top 3 actions:
1.
2.
3.

Making habits stick

We all have good intentions, but in practice most resolutions never stick. I often coach managers who have set ambitious goals and then feel disappointed in themselves because they have not achieved them. Here is my advice:

> To attain the goals you set, you need to incorporate them one by one into your daily routine, so they become habits. Habits are actions that we do automatically each day without even thinking about them, e.g. cleaning our teeth, brushing our hair, etc. – they become part of our daily routine.

Here are some tips on how to make a goal a habit:

1. Implement your goals one at a time.
2. Start with the easiest goal.
3. Write it down – you are more likely to do it.
4. Start simple – make the desired action easy to do.
5. Do it each day for the next 30 days – this will ensure that it is incorporated into your daily routine.
6. Do it initially for five minutes a day. Start small and gradually increase the time you spend on the activity each day.
7. Find a trigger to prompt you to do the activity. 'Piggyback' a new habit onto an old one. For example, do five minutes of stretching after you clean your teeth.
8. Be consistent – do the activity at the same time and in the same place each day.

To keep yourself motivated to continue to implement your goal:

1. Set yourself a calendar reminder about the goal two weeks after the start.
2. Review after two weeks what you have achieved, the inner resources you have used to achieve this and how you can use these to keep going.
3. Find a buddy to help and encourage you.
4. Identify a role model who displays the desired behaviour and consider what you can learn from them.
5. List the benefits of attaining your goal.
6. Visualise yourself succeeding.
7. Be kind to yourself – no one is perfect. If you fall short of your goal, think: "what can I learn from this?"
8. Celebrate success!

Quotes on resilience

"Do not judge me by my success, judge me by how many times I fell down and got back up again."

Nelson Mandela

"I can be changed by what happens to me. But I refuse to be reduced by it."

Maya Angelou

"It is your reaction to adversity, not adversity itself, that determines how your life's story will develop."

Dieter F. Uchtdorf

"Rock bottom became the solid foundation on which I rebuilt my life."

J.K. Rowling

9: Conclusion and making habits stick

Best wishes for the continued development of your resilience.

Sarah Cook

sarah@thestairway.co.uk

FURTHER READING

IT Governance Publishing (ITGP) is the world's leading publisher for governance and compliance. Our industry-leading pocket guides, books, training resources and toolkits are written by real-world practitioners and thought leaders. They are used globally by audiences of all levels, from students to C-suite executives.

Our high-quality publications cover all IT governance, risk and compliance frameworks and are available in a range of formats. This ensures our customers can access the information they need in the way they need it.

Our other soft skills publications include:

- *Making a Success of Managing and Working Remotely* by Sarah Cook, *www.itgovernancepublishing.co.uk/product/making-a-success-of-managing-and-working-remotely*
- *Building a High-Performance Team – Proven techniques for effective team working* by Sarah Cook, *www.itgovernancepublishing.co.uk/product/building-a-high-performance-team*
- *Changing how you manage and communicate change – Focusing on the human side of change* by Naomi Karten, *www.itgovernancepublishing.co.uk/product/changing-how-you-manage-and-communicate-change*

For more information on ITGP and branded publishing services, and to view our full list of publications, visit *www.itgovernancepublishing.co.uk*.

To receive regular updates from ITGP, including information on new publications in your area(s) of interest, sign up for our newsletter at *www.itgovernancepublishing.co.uk/topic/newsletter*.

Branded publishing

Through our branded publishing service, you can customise ITGP publications with your company's branding.

Find out more at *www.itgovernancepublishing.co.uk/topic/branded-publishing-services*.

Related services

ITGP is part of GRC International Group, which offers a comprehensive range of complementary products and services to help organisations meet their objectives.

For a full range of GCR International Group's resources visit *www.itgovernance.co.uk*.

Training services

The IT Governance training programme is built on our extensive practical experience designing and implementing management systems based on ISO standards, best practice and regulations.

Our courses help attendees develop practical skills and comply with contractual and regulatory requirements. They also support career development via recognised qualifications.

Learn more about our training courses and view the full course catalogue at *www.itgovernance.co.uk/training*.

Professional services and consultancy

We are a leading global consultancy of IT governance, risk management and compliance solutions. We advise businesses around the world on their most critical issues and present cost-saving and risk-reducing solutions based on international best practice and frameworks.

We offer a wide range of delivery methods to suit all budgets, timescales and preferred project approaches.

Find out how our consultancy services can help your organisation at *www.itgovernance.co.uk/consulting*.

Industry news

Want to stay up to date with the latest developments and resources in the IT governance and compliance market? Subscribe to our Weekly Round-up newsletter and we will send you mobile-friendly emails with fresh news and features about your preferred areas of interest, as well as unmissable offers and free resources to help you successfully start your projects. *www.itgovernance.co.uk/weekly-round-up*.

EU for product safety is Stephen Evans, The Mill Enterprise Hub, Stagreenan, Drogheda, Co. Louth, A92 CD3D, Ireland. (servicecentre@itgovernance.eu)